Sister Stan's book of
Inspirations

Sr Stanislaus Kennedy

SISTER STAN's book of
INSPIRATIONS

the columba press

First published in 2012 by

the columba press

55A Spruce Avenue,
Stillorgan Industrial Park,
Blackrock, Co. Dublin
www.columba.ie

ISBN 978 1 78218 220 7

Design by Emer O Boyle
and David Mc Namara CSsR

Printed by ScandBook AB

The Sanctuary, a meditation centre in the heart of Dublin city, was founded in 1998 by Sr Stanislaus Kennedy. It has been evolving around its vision – to be … STILLNESS … in the world. The Sanctuary believes that everyone – the child, the teenager, the adult – can access this place of stillness within themselves and that once it is part of their consciousness, its potential for their well-being and the well-being of society is huge.

www.sanctuary.ie

INTRODUCTION

This little book is meant for everyone who wishes to read it. It isn't written to convince you about anything. It is a book to have by your side, in your bag, in your pocket or at your bedside. Pick it up and put it down as you please.

It is not a book to be read sequentially. It is not about bringing you new ideas that you might play around with, analyse or criticise. Read the reflections and aphorisms in your own way and in your own time. Allow them to speak to your heart; to create a silence within you; to reveal their message to you; to draw you ever more deeply into the journey of life. It is simply intended that this little book will bring you into a deeper part of your being, the still point where Thomas Merton has said:

'God has written his name on us.'

JANUARY

JANUARY

I   Moments of stillness, moments of silence,
connect us with the whole of life.

—·—

2   Each dawn a genesis, a new beginning, a
resurrection, a promise.

—·—

3   Snow – a painted landscape
calling me to stillness.

—·—

4   Creation speaks to our hearts
when we listen.

Standing on the shore, part of the rhythm
of the tide. Each wave a giving and a taking,
impermanence dissolving into permanence.

5

The journey of the river is like the journey of
the soul, feeding itself from its own source.

6

The bounty of the universe begins with
the gift of life.

7

Nature: we are part of it, living it,
breathing it. It is part of us,
encompassing us, holding us in its heart.

8

9   A flower opening to morning light,
closing as the light fades: a daily miracle.

---

10   The material world is our way to contact
divine life; every tiny little bit of it a
glimpse into the soul of eternity.

---

11   Surrendering completely to sound we
discover sacred stillness.

---

12   Life is a series of experiences through which
we can come to know our true selves.

When we acknowledge another with full and
unconditional attention we meet ourselves.

13

Maturity combines the fresh enthusiasm of
youth with the wisdom of age.

14

Joy comes in little whispers, in sudden
unexpected glimpses.

15

Memories are our greatest treasure,
always present in any space,
in every place.

16

JANUARY

17
The more we discover the more
we have to learn.

———

18
Our search is ongoing,
our journey unfinished.

———

19
Every step on our journey is
a return to the beginning.

———

20
In learning not to fear uncertainty we
discover inner strength.

When I know that enough is enough
I will have enough always.

21

———

Our unlived lives, our undreamt
dreams, our greatest loss is the life we
allow to die while we live.

22

———

Life is simple and serene when it is
lived from the heart with integrity.

23

———

The beginning and end of our journey
is finding our true selves.

24

25   Living life is not automatic:
     we must choose to live it.

26   Living with integrity, we bring body,
     mind and spirit into everything.

27   Courage is a gift of the heart. It opens us to
     experience, stirs us to compassion,
     and frees our creativity.

28   Life is about giving and receiving,
     moment by moment.

Our humanity calls us in our poverty
to make the world a better place.

29

A life of love is a choice we make.

30

We all long to feel real, yet we fear it.
We run away even as we are
irresistibly drawn to it.

31

FEBRUARY

FEBRUARY

1 Neighbourliness: a sacred gift
in a torn world.

———

2 There is another way to live in this noisy,
distracted world and it is not as out of
reach as it may seem.

———

3 There is no limit to wakefulness: no one
wakes up once and for all.

———

4 To live from the heart is to love fully.

The purpose of this day is to discover
who we are and what we are called to be.

5

The purpose of this day is to find the joy
we are born to know.

6

It is only in losing ourselves that we find
our true selves.

7

The wonder moments of life keep our
hearts alive and sustain us in dark times.

8

9 All life is connected at the core, flowing from
   the same source – the divine river of life.

———

10 In the here, in the now – an eternal moment.

———

11 Living in the moment we do not
    miss the present.

———

12 Our destiny is here, it is now.

Mindfulness is an inner structure,
sensitised to the now.

13

We cannot reach the now if we think of
it in a chronological way.

14

We do not own time, gain or save it.
All we can do is live it.

15

We enter into the now in our most alive
moments when time stands still.

16

FEBRUARY

17   Eternity is the overcoming of time by
the now that does not pass away.

---

18   When we live in the moment
we live in and out of time.

---

19   We are reborn each day, into a new time
with a new opportunity to respond to
yesterday's difficulties.

---

20   When we listen to the silence of the
moment we hear the deep desires and
longings of our heart.

FEBRUARY

When we let time go, time is ours.   21

Eternity is in our heart, calling us home.   22

Time, through which life passes, is a
divine freedom empowering us now.   23

When we open our eyes with gratitude
the world is filled with light.   24

25

Believing what is not seen, seeing what
is not visible, knowing the limits
of our life, we give thanks.

⸺∞⸺

26

Giving and receiving are one in gratitude:
we cannot give thanks for what we
have not taken to heart.

⸺∞⸺

27

Gratitude always gives more.

⸺∞⸺

28

At the core of our being is emptiness and
fullness, nothingness and everything;
there dwells the divine.

When we allow surprise to flow in our
lives, we take nothing for granted.

29

MARCH

MARCH

1   A grateful heart is a heart filled with joy.

—❦—

2   The child in us never dies.

—❦—

3   Gratefulness is being surprised
by the ordinary.

—❦—

4   Every moment is given,
every moment a gift.

Dignity is never diminished
by indifference or ill will.

5

Absorbed in lighting a candle, watching
the flame flickering, we enter into the
stillness of the small circle of light.

6

Beauty is found in solitude, in nature
and in the unfolding of the human heart.

7

Only in stillness do we hear truth.
Only through stillness do we understand truth.
Only out of stillness do we speak truth.

8

9

The soul is that place in us where
love and light, joy and peace,
truth and beauty abide.

10

Awake, aware, beyond thought,
pure presence – stillness.

11

We are infinitely more than we imagine,
infinitely greater than our mind.

12

The spiritual life is a life of love, a life of
giving and receiving. It is never a solo act.

Living by measurements, achievements, ambitions, goals and expectations, we forget when enough is enough.

13

It takes courage to follow the deepest desires of our heart, to say no to other people's plans for us, to leave other voices behind and to say yes to the quiet, still voice calling from within.

14

Whenever anyone responds with love or kindness, wherever anyone seeks truth, peace or justice, there God is.

15

God is always at work in us, even this very moment. What fluctuates is our openness and receptivity.

16

17   To be full, we must be empty.

18   Letting go of the compulsion to be
successful, to be right, to be in control,
to be powerful, is the only way to freedom.

19   We can only take with us when we die
what we let go when we are alive.

20   In letting go of life, we discover new life.

Ours is the choice – to live in trust
or live in fear.

21

We can overcome our fear only
by letting go of it.

22

Absorbed in ourselves, unaware of what
life is offering, we are unable to receive
the joys of the moment, the gifts of today.

23

Entering into the night, we return into
the silence that is the dark soil in which
we are rooted.

24

25   The less we have,
the easier it is to appreciate.

———

26   If we learn to let go during life we will
be able to die easily.

———

27   Any time is a time to stop, live in the
moment and accept what is.

———

28   Indecision, holding back, standing on
the edge of fear, breeds insecurity.

When we live a detached life,
pretending to be something we are not,   29
we cannot live at ease with ourselves.

When we accept our weakness
everything changes. The mirage of   30
control disappears and our
weakness becomes our strength.

Night completes the circle of the hours   31
as death completes the circle of life.

APRIL

APURL

To let go, to be able to stand and leave
everything behind without looking back,
is to say yes to inner freedom.

1

———

At birth, we are given an angel,
a gift of courage. All we need to know
is that it is there.

2

———

Life is a river and if we learn to let go, not
to cling to the banks, just to go with the
flow, it carries us; it bears us up in trust.

3

———

Death is the way into the divine presence,
the resolution of a lifetime of wonder
and waiting.

4

Learning to be present to the present:
Serenity.

5

—∞—

Living is letting go. The mother lets go
of her child so that the child can enter
fully into life.

6

—∞—

In meditation we let go of everything –
the outer world of the senses, the inner world
of thought – and listen to the still voice within.

7

—∞—

Little deaths accepted bring
new life and inner peace.

8

9   This is one of the basic laws of life –
that when we give we receive.

———

10   As we connect, reconnect and interconnect,
our lives are woven into unity.

———

11   Tomorrow is the enemy of today,
for we cannot be tomorrow
what we can be today.

———

12   Without love, justice is realism,
hope is self-centredness,
forgiveness is self-abasement,
generosity is extravagance.

When we journey with awareness, each
event is unique, each step is the first step.

13

When we hear the stillness in the heart
of the world, all creation becomes
our companion.

14

In stillness I notice people around me,
who they are, who I am, where we are
going, how we journey together.

15

Music arises out of silence
into which it inevitably flows.

16

17 Joy is the experience of losing ourselves,
of being emptied of self.

———

18 Prayer is attuning ourselves
to the flow of life.

———

19 Sitting still, trying not to try, wanting
not to want, not setting our heart on
anything, we discover inner peace.

———

20 Prayer changes us and in changing us
it changes the world.

When I stop, I find you. When I look, I
see you. When I listen, I hear you.

21

—◦◦◦—

Prayer is not working or straining the mind;
it is a simple matter of opening the heart.

22

—◦◦◦—

This is how we learn to be still: by sitting
quietly, facing fear with trust, listening to
our own depth, allowing the dawn to rise
out of the night.

23

—◦◦◦—

Peace is found not only in the desert or
in some remote and silent monastery
but in the tumult of the marketplace and
the pulse of the human heart.

24

25   Prayer is never a private matter. It is always inclusive. It is opening our hearts to the universe.

26   Stillness accepts noise; then moves beneath it to an inner silence.

27   You are always in and around me, always sheltering me, but it is only in awareness that I experience you.

28   We are one, you and I, bound together in a covenant of peace, ringed around in a circle of love.

Silently listening to our breathing,
we are intimately at one
with the life breath of the universe.

29

When we are too busy to be still our ears
and eyes are open only to projects and plans,
missing the wonder of the moment.

30

MAY

MAY

I   Forgiveness is a taste of divine grace –
a pure gift.

—◆◆◆—

2   Preserving the silence within amid all
the noise and clatter of life, we grow into
our true selves.

—◆◆◆—

3   Prayer is an opening of the heart that
takes us beyond our limited rational
mind, beyond the ego, the separate self,
into the transcendent mystery.

—◆◆◆—

4   Each morning blesses us with time and space
to be attentive to all that is new this day.

When the challenges of the day overwhelm us
they can also remind us to stop,
to catch our breath, to make sense,
to take rest, to find strength in the moment.

5

Before we sleep, gathering up all the
day's contradictions, knitting together
what is broken – a healing experience.

6

Life is about moments.

7

Receptivity: a condition of the night, a
reminder of the often unrecognised
virtue of lives lived in dependency, of
lives lived in the service of others.

8

9   Setting aside our day we enter serenity.

---

10   Opening to our inner self frees us to
trust each new moment in time.

---

11   Before turning on the computer,
opening the door, getting into the car,
answering the phone, let us stop, pause
and breathe, mindfully.

---

12   Mortality reminds us to do what we do well;
happily, joyfully, freely living in the now.

Each dawn a gift,
moving out of darkness into light.

13

Aspiring to be good,
we inspire others to goodness.

14

There is never a moment that isn't an
opportunity to make space for the new
by letting go of the old.

15

Realising our potential,
our gifts shine out as blessings.

16

17
Pondering in our hearts creation's story,
surrendering to the rhythms of the day
and the night, we savour the now.

18
Silence embraced, truth and beauty
become visible.

19
The wise composer allows music to
crescendo, reach a climax and then –
pause, rest, silence, nothing. In the
silence, we hear the music.

20
No one lives by chance. Everyone,
everything has a purpose, a part to play
in the grand design that is creation.

Being alive is sufficient proof that we
are essential to all creation, to all time.

21

A day lived in unity with nature
is a day flowing in the eternal
interconnectedness of creation.

22

Our purpose this day is not finding
security and certainty, it is discovering
the very best that is within us.

23

Learning to trust ourselves, following
our deepest desires, exploring the
recesses of our heart we become whole.

24

25 The purpose of this day is to discover
and accept who we are and what we are
called to be.

26 Our spiritual journey –
the greatest human adventure.

27 The silence of the night invites us to
detach ourselves from the possession of
the day, entrusting it and ourselves
to the freedom of God.

28 In detachment from things we are free
from small-mindedness.

In practising awareness we learn to
take possession of ourselves.

29

In letting go we learn to live with
ambiguity.

30

In living with questions we learn to
wait for answers.

31

JUNE

JUNE

I

Patient waiting in silence teaches us to believe
in ourselves and transform problems
into possibilities.

———

2

Night-time: examining the day,
being grateful, forgiving,
confronting our fears.
Looking back, we lean forward.

———

3

Learning to accept and live with polarities,
tensions, paradoxes and contradictions is
the secret to wholeness.

———

4

Accepting without understanding,
honouring differences, finding unity in
diversity we move into truth.

Being mindful, giving thanks for what is given we bring to mind what otherwise might go unnoticed.

5

Giving thanks, we become less concerned with what is missing and more focused on sharing what we have.

6

As a musician, athlete, dancer benefits from the discipline of routine, so we too – through a daily spiritual routine – will unfold and blossom with vitality, joy and sensitivity.

7

The way of truth tests our heart, examines our motivation, challenges our commitment, and always bears fruit.

8

9   With gratitude we make peace with our
     world and everything in our life.

———

10   Time in the evening connecting with
     ourselves and the splendour of the
     universe, we are transformed.

———

11   When we are challenged to stay on the road,
     not to turn back, to trust our inner wisdom,
     we touch that sacred space within.

———

12   Joy cannot be organised, cannot be
     planned. We need only desire it,
     seek it and it finds us.

Aware or unaware, we create our own
solutions, our own reality by choice
or by chance.

13

Joy is ours when we do what we really
want to do in freedom and integrity
of heart.

14

At the core of our being we are all one,
as we touch and are touched by each other.

15

A life taken for granted never knows joy.

16

JUNE

17 Accepting the mystery of our being –
not proving it but being it – we become
the self we were born to be.

·····

18 Creation: ongoing story, new
beginnings, nothing complete.

·····

19 Creation: always becoming, always
being shaped, never complete.

·····

20 Truth comes in pairs of opposites.

We are strong when we embrace our
weaknesses, we are teachers when we
can be taught.

21

We enjoy others when we enjoy ourselves;
when we enjoy ourselves, we are wise.

22

When we accept our own foolishness,
we find true happiness.

23

Many of us become what others
tell us we are.

24

25 Listening to the small voice within we
discover the person we are called to be,
in our delightful uniqueness.

—◆—

26 Living in the moment,
we experience life.

—◆—

27 In stillness a flower blooms,
in stillness it fades away.

—◆—

28 Moving out of darkness into light,
a moment neither dark nor light,
a time to delight.

Morning: birth of colour, leaf and flower
newly risen, out of the night, out of the earth,   29
leaving the darkness without regret.

Growth happens in the fertile darkness
where the rain falls and the seed opens   30
no matter how many trample overhead.

JULY

JULY

1

The last darkness of night dissipates,
the sun bursts over the horizon –
every day a new miracle –
rarely experienced, yet always there.

2

Darkness before dawn,
pregnant with light.

3

The treasures of the earth are free
and full of surprises.

4

The earth speaks in magic –
rainbows and waterfalls speak to the heart.

In accepting the inevitability of death we
discover a new way of living.

5

———

Life fuelling the universe, always
flowing into us, blessing us; flowing
through us, blessing others.

6

———

It is in responding with a full heart
that we experience joy.

7

———

Divine joy is in us, given to us out of
love, being born in us anew each day.

8

9

Work dignifies our every day,
enabling what is unlived in us to flower.

———

10

The world is ever being created, each
of us in the making as each moment
we are transformed in love.

———

11

Unlike other creatures, we struggle to
become who we are, as we experience
ourselves unfinished.

———

12

When we face challenges,
we find meaning.

The harvest of our lives is already within.   13

With every gift comes opportunities.
Enjoying them to the full,   14
we rejoice in the gift of being alive.

Time does not run out.
It rises as water in a well,   15
to fullness.

Only here in this moment
is the mystery of now.   16

17

Bells: a timeless call to enter the now,
to stop, to listen, to hear the message
of this moment and give thanks.

18

Dying daily, we move naturally
into eternal life.

19

Living in the now is an invitation to
awaken our souls, to stop, to listen, to
choose a different way.

20

When we turn the point between time
and now into creative tension,
we live life to the fullest.

We think we have no time,
that we are running out of time,
that time is out of our control.   21
But time is eternal, and we have all the time
we need, always, because all time is ours, now.

Thank you for the ordinary gifts of every day,
evoking in me wonder and surprise.   22

Praise is our response to glory. The more
open we are, the more glory shines out.   23

Just for ten seconds in silence remember those
who loved the good that grows within us, those
who wanted what was best for us, those who   24
encouraged us to become who we are.

JULY

25   It is not enough to feel grateful –
we must think gratefully, imagine
gratefully, act gratefully.

———

26   In giving we are replenished.

———

27   Teach me to wait silently, untroubled
and without fear but full of gratitude.

———

28   We are blessed when we are open
to the gifts of the day.

Gratitude is an attitude making us alive
to what we have.

29

Surprise cannot be planned or controlled
but it is always there when we
are open to it.

30

Just as we see the sun in its rays, the
fountain in its waters, so we can see
the streams of divine power in the daily
graces flowing into our lives.

31

AUGUST

AUGUST

1 A soul touched by the Spirit is like a tree touched by the sun.

---

2 Creation, beginning of time, before time, in time, all time.

---

3 Soul is the unifying force at the centre of our being, never changing in a constantly changing world.

---

4 The divine is the depth dimension in human experience.

Journeying in faith we are who we are in
God – no more, no less.

5

⸺⚬⚬⚬⚬⸺

A flame burning, snowflake falling, bud
opening, wheel spinning –
the dynamic of stillness.

6

⸺⚬⚬⚬⚬⸺

Divine grace is like a lantern on a dark path –
shining only to illuminate the next step.

7

⸺⚬⚬⚬⚬⸺

Connecting with the spirit we open ourselves
to the force that drives the universe.

8

9　　Spirituality integrates and transforms
the material world.

⸺⸙⸺

10　　We need to learn to let go of ourselves
and in letting go we find God in our
heart's core.

⸺⸙⸺

11　　Reflecting on the brokenness and fragility
of our day, we greet the silence
of the night.

⸺⸙⸺

12　　Each moment, I am one with the force
of life.

Letting go, we open ourselves
to what is given.

13

Detachment: accepting life, accepting
ourselves as we are, our giftedness
and our limitations.

14

As we move towards death,
we grow into it, day by day.

15

Detachment leads us out, beyond ourselves,
connecting us into the universe.

16

17   The moment we die to ourselves is the
     moment we are fully alive.

---

18   The word that we are is always in the
     process of being spoken, completed
     only in death.

---

19   When we rise wholeheartedly to the
     challenges of the day we will be let go
     when it is time to leave it all behind.

---

20   Blessed, we bless in our turn,
     in our way, on our way.

By faith we die forward into the
fullness of life and that is resurrection.

21

———

Knowing light shines in the dark,
we come to know darkness itself as light.

22

———

God is in the mountain. The mountain
is in God. I am in the mountain, and
the mountain is in me.

23

———

The soul of the world is the pulse of the
unfathomable, the heartbeat of all creation,
mysterious, sacred beyond words.

24

25

Through you I rise –
and you through me –
into this new day we are making together.

26

Evening, when we have forgotten how
to pray, it is enough to give ourselves
over, in trust, to the night.

27

In night prayer we connect the end of
the day with the end of life.

28

True living means alive to God,
alive to ourselves and alive to others.

When we see with the heart,
we discover that there is no part of life
that doesn't contain a surprise.

29

We live in a changing world –
if we don't change we die.

30

Moments of stillness and peace are always
available. They are offered to everyone.
It is only a matter of being aware.

31

SEPTEMBER

SEPTEMBER

1
Remember, until you love yourself in small ways, you cannot change yourself in bigger ways.

2
Accepting our limitations, we experience a new freedom and a new serenity.

3
The difficulties, tensions, pressures of the commuter's morning, dissipate at a glimpse of the morning sky.

4
Instead of wanting more, give thanks for the blessings you already have.

Through our compassion,
we too can change the world.

5

Our inner beauty flows through our
eyes, our smiles, our expressions, our
gestures, our perceptions, our joy, our
care and our compassion.

6

Take the time to stop, look, observe.
Beauty surrounds you.

7

Nourish your body with healthy food and
exercise. Nourish your mind with good
literature, art and company.
Nourish your spirit with silence,
stillness and prayer.

8

9   Do not be concerned about things you cannot change. Concern yourself, rather, with what you can.

—◦◦◦—

10   If you recognise and do well what is needed today, the future will find you doing what is needed at that time.

—◦◦◦—

11   The present moment is all you are sure of. Living in the moment is living fully.

—◦◦◦—

12   Always wanting to be right closes the mind and heart. With an open mind and an open heart, we may not always be right, but we won't be wrong.

Moments when we bless and feel blessed
are moments when we are most alone,   13
yet most alive to everyone and everything.

If we try not to look ahead to tomorrow,
but instead live today well,   14
tomorrow will be happier.

Seeing with the mind, we see possibilities
and potential. Seeing with the heart,
we have insights into life's   15
deepest meanings.

Rid yourself of anxiety and anger.
Learn to walk with joy.   16
Enjoy yourself and your own company.

17   Hope is promise. Hope is possibility. Hope is about what is not yet. Hope is about what you do not see, but you trust is there.

---

18   Carrying bags of anger and resentment takes a lot of energy. Forgive, and you will immediately feel lighter.

---

19   Each moment is the place you arrive at from your most recent past and from which you step into the future.

---

20   If we surrender to difficult situations, we develop new ways of living. We learn to hold what happens. We learn to deal with it. We learn to learn from it.

Busyness can keep you from receiving
the joy of the moment, the joy of the day.

21

Life is a gift that comes wrapped
in what you experience.

22

A rainbow, a pure gift, comes quite
unexpectedly, apparently from nowhere –
an invitation to stop and stare.

23

An easy ride can't teach you how to
handle a dangerous, bumpy road.

24

25 Forgive yourself, forgive others, and you will live your life as a free human being.

---

26 Through listening, you can learn how to rise above adversity, and learn to truly value other people who are very different from you.

---

27 Patience is the skill of understanding and respecting our own rhythms and those of others.

---

28 No matter how painful life may be, we have internal resources to heal and grow into happiness.

Peace comes from the heart that knows
that all life is sacred and all human   29
beings are equal.

What we see or presume to see, day after
day, constitutes who we are and colours   30
our whole life.

OCTOBER

OCTOBER

I

When you really live in hope,
you do not deny darkness or negativity
or pain, but neither do you give in
or resign yourself to it.

—∞—

2

It is impossible to know who you are
unless you know where you belong.

—∞—

3

Happiness comes from loving yourself
as you are.

—∞—

4

If your view is tired and stale, if
everything you see appears empty, maybe
it is because you yourself are empty.

Attention is the medium through
which kindness flows.

5

—◦◦◦—

Kindness and compassion are sources
of lasting happiness and joy, the
foundations of a loving heart.

6

—◦◦◦—

Life is created when you trust in the
promise of unseen things, just as buds
hold life in the depth of winter.

7

—◦◦◦—

Accepting people we meet as they are is
a practice that keeps our hearts open.

8

9 Resentment is a barrier to our growth.
Forgiveness is the beginning of our freedom.

———

10 Living in the now challenges our tendency
to wait or delay until success is
assured before beginning.

———

11 Knowing a person's story softens our
judgement, makes us more tolerant,
and leads to peace.

———

12 Night prayer: drawing us into the
mystery of night. We gather our day,
offering it back to God in gratitude.

All the elements for your happiness
are already here, just be.

13

Without happiness we cannot be
a refuge for others.

14

Hope encourages us to follow our dreams,
to believe in that part of us that
envisions a new way.

15

Life is for living.

16

OCTOBER

17
Everything has its time,
and that is always now.

18
When we become more individualistic,
we become more isolated.

19
Self-esteem, once truly acquired
can never be lost.

20
The acknowledgement of
impermanence is the key to life itself.

Life unfolds everywhere at its own pace.　21

Prophets are people with their feet on
the ground, but with their minds and　22
hearts filled with fiery dreams.

It is by facing our wounds
that we discover what it is　23
that gives our lives meaning.

Old age, the harvest time of life,
a time to gather experiences,
to celebrate them,　24
and to share them.

25
Being honest about our struggles,
our fears and our hopes are the best gift
we can pass on to others.

26
Deep within each of us there is a
knowing place. When we spend time there,
we tend to the gifts that we have been given,
we discover how fruitful our life has been
and how much we can share with the world.

27
The reaper in us lives and works out of
love with no assurance of success.

28
Now is the time for us to reach out
and see beauty in life's becoming.

Some visions unfold in our sleep, some
in visionary, waking moments. Seizing
these moments, we dream new dreams.

29

When our heart breaks out of its
protective shell we feel naked.
It is in this nakedness that we taste
the essential nature of our existence.

30

The earth's whispers are everywhere,
but only those who have slept and
dreamt with it can respond to its call.

31

NOVEMBER

I

Solitude is not running away. Rather,
solitude helps us to create communion,
by taking others into our hearts,
into our solitude.

———

2

The more deeply we listen, the more we
tune ourselves into the cry of our heart.

———

3

It is only if we choose to be attentive that
we open our hearts to the wonder of things.

———

4

It is a strange paradox that the more we
forget ourselves, the more we find ourselves.

The virtue of attentiveness allows us to enjoy the journey and the destination.

5

When we let go of our time, all time is ours because we are in the present moment, in the now that transcends time.

6

All we need is to be, to be present, to believe, to love, to trust, because God is breathing on us and through us.

7

Moving from a place of stillness, we are capable of having a right understanding, making right judgements and taking right actions.

8

NOVEMBER

9 Hope doesn't need words or proofs or conditions. Hope accepts mystery and offers the gift of solid trust in the unknown.

---

10 Simplicity clears our vision and allows us to see what we really need and what is really enough.

---

11 Negativity is a great clutterer. It keeps us from receiving the joys of the moment, the joys of the day.

---

12 While it is essential that we become more loving persons, it is equally important that we accept ourselves as we really are.

We live a simple life when we do not
pretend to be something we are not.

13

To unclutter our lives is to open our
hearts, to create emptiness where
fullness becomes possible.

14

Today we can give away something we
treasure which would enrich the life of
somebody else and liberate ours.

15

The greatest gift we can bring to another
is to open up to them their hidden
reservoir of love.

16

17 Evening: a time to reflect on what we
need, what we can let go, and what we
can gather together before moving on.

18 The heart stands for the centre of our
being, where we are at one with ourselves,
one with others, and one with that pure spirit
of love that some of us call God.

19 The loss of a loved one is a gap in the heart
forever, because a door in our life closes
that can never be opened by anyone else.

20 No matter how close we get to one another,
you can never know what it is like to be me
and I can never know what it is like to be you.

The journey of self-knowledge and
self-acceptance is finding and accepting   21
the great mystery that we are.

This is the struggle of a lifetime,
accepting the me within whom lies great   22
beauty and great possibilities.

It is precisely at the point of acceptance
of our fragility and our brokenness that true   23
development and growth can take place.

The greater our awareness of each
moment, the more we can let go of the   24
stories that control our life.

25

The less we assume, the more we are surprised and delighted with what we discover in the world.

26

The surprise of the unexpected will wear off, but the surprise of freshness never wears off.

27

When compassion becomes the foundation of our attitude to others, we see them with a fresh gaze and an open heart.

28

There is plenty for all of us – for you and for me – if only we have the eyes to see and the ears to hear and the heart to feel the gifts within us and around us.

The way to heal a greedy, envious or
demanding heart is to replace it
with a grateful heart.

29

When we are grateful, our lives will begin
to change instantly and we will see clearly.

30

DECEMBER

DECEMBER

1

In giving gifts, we often give what we
can spare, but in giving thanks,
we give ourselves.

2

Even if our life lacks the surprise
of the extraordinary, the ordinary
can always be surprising.

3

Tenderness does not mean sentimentality;
rather, it is unearthing gentleness and kindness,
which shows that we consider other people
to be important and precious.

4

Our forgiveness may not always be
accepted, but once we have reached out
our hand we rid ourselves of resentment.

If we cannot live at peace amidst the problems of our daily surroundings, we're not likely to make peace with the significant wounds and traumas of our life.

5

If we are successful in the denial of our pain, we create the illusion that it is under control. But that is not healing; it is merely temporary containment.

6

We can only bring compassion to others if we have experienced it ourselves.

7

One spurt of surprise can lead to a blaze of gratefulness.

8

9

It is important to hold memories of goodness,
to draw from them the goodness in us;
to catch it, to dwell on it, to savour it.

10

As we walk life's journey, realising that
we are connected with all that has gone
before and all that is present, we are
preparing for what is to come.

11

Many of us are just flickering wicks that
need to be pared and cared for, very
gently, carefully and confidently.

12

Peace comes when we have met and
accepted the best and the worst within us.

When we know what goes on in our
own heart we become more accepting,   13
tolerant and more open.

We can only become peace-filled people
if we first acknowledge our own   14
propensity to violence and learn from it.

If we are in harmony with ourselves,
we are in harmony with the movement   15
of the whole universe.

When we smile, life is good and goodness
is all around us and that makes us more gentle   16
with ourselves and with others.

DECEMBER

17 Whether we are conscious of it or not, we all carry responsibility for the good and evil in our world today.

---

18 Learning more about the great poverty and brokenness of our lives, we are also learning more about our potential and strength and the source of it.

---

19 When we are too caught up with our projects and programmes, we miss out on the important things, our inner resources.

---

20 Hope is living our dreams even when we experience failure and self-doubt.

Loss in nature is also loss for humanity,
and we are all responsible for maintaining
the harmony of the universe.

21

The pain of life accepted with courage
awakens our love, stirs our compassion,
opens our mind – a gift of the heart.

22

There is nothing – no person, no thing,
no thought, no experience, no sadness or joy –
nothing too small or nothing too great that
cannot be gathered and used for the
nourishment and beauty and good of all.

23

Being people of light and hope means
being willing to stay open to our fears.

24

DECEMBER

25 Wisdom is not knowing as well as knowing, and being at peace with that uncertainty.

---

26 Some of us have a blind hardness that quickly surfaces when our patch is threatened. It is prayer that softens our hardened hearts.

---

27 When we dare to see with the eyes of the soul, we begin to see sharper images, and our intuitive powers grow.

---

28 Life is an art. The art lies not in what we experience in life – but in how we harmonise our experiences.

Just before sunrise the world takes a
deep breath, a crescendo of twitters
salute the day.

29

Dawn chorus, exhaling new life
echoing over the earth.

30

Pause, reflect, catch your breath,
make peace, find joy – in the moment.

31